CREATIONS
of
WONDER

Alex M. Frame MSc, Th.D.

ISBN 978-1-965679-65-4 (Paperback)
ISBN 978-1-965679-66-1 (Ebook)

Inquiries and Book Orders should be addressed to:

Leavitt Peak Press
17901 Pioneer Blvd Ste L #298, Artesia, California 90701
Phone #: 2092191548

Acknowledgements

All biblical scripture is taken from the King James Authorised version.

**To
Lisa**

Preface

The opening statement of the whole Bible is 'In the beginning, God created', and this creator God has the incarnate image of Jesus Christ of whom is said that 'all things were created through Him and for Him' (Colossians 1:15–16).

This can be seen to be so far removed from much of today's teachings, like that of evolution and its propounder, Charles Darwin. The Theory of Evolution is in truth exactly what it says it is, a *theory*, and it raises many more questions than answers.

If we are to believe in God's word and what He says, then creation and evolution of species are incompatible. It is not the purpose of this book to prove creation, although the writer would have no difficulty in this, but it is simply to highlight some of these creations that are seen as not just the wonders of creation, but rather the creations of wonder.

As for Darwin, who studied theology for three years at Cambridge to become a minister of the gospel, he never denied the Almighty God. On his deathbed, he requested his visitor, one Lady Hope, to hold a meeting in his summerhouse and to invite his servants, tenants, and neighbours to come. When she asked, 'What shall I speak about?' Darwin replied, 'Christ and His salvation. Is not that the best theme?'

The word *create* means more than just 'make', for we can all do that. But to make something out of nothing, that is real creation. Therefore, we could say that anything created is wonderful, and so indeed it is. Yet within the host of creation, there are some things that, when viewed more closely, stand apart as extra special.

This book is about a mere handful of these creations, culminating in man himself and the one devastating 'creation' of that man – the cross of death.

The Lily of the Field

Consider the lilies of the field, how they grow; they toil not, neither do they spin, and yet I say unto you that even Solomon, in all his glory, was not arrayed like one of these. —Matthew 6:28–29

It would be true to say that we do not know the precise flower that Jesus had in mind when we read this passage, or indeed that He meant any particular flower, or that He was merely referring to the general showing of the wildflowers.

There have been many comments, opinions, and discussions as to which flower Jesus was alluding to. There are many variations in the lily family.

There is the Crown Imperial white lily, which is not usually found in a wild state in Israel; the Star of Bethlehem, a white flower that blooms in springtime; and the Hyacinth, which is a perennial having blue flowers that also shows in the springtime.

There is the greenish, bell-like, drooping flower belonging to the Lebanon Fritillary, and a rare lily called the Forest Squill, which has a beautiful delicate flower of white and blue and can be seen in mountain areas and slopes.

Many have thought that the lily spoken about is the flower that grows in hidden and sheltered clifftop places, and they have named it the Madonna Lily. Then again, there is the Sea Squill, which is, as its name suggests, a coastal plant. This lily grows tall, with spikes yielding white flowers and poisonous bulbs. Along the coastal sands also grows the Sea Lily, which has large white flowers that, although they are very beautiful, last for only a day.

The Mountain Lily is a perennial daffodil of the lily family with blue flowers, and it is found on the mountain slopes. In the dry places, a flower belonging to the lily family is the Desert Tulip, which is very prominent with its bright red flowers.

Perhaps the lily best known in the Holy Land is the Narcissus, which is probably the Lily of the Valley spoken about in the Song of Solomon 2:1. It is a perennial flower found all over in fields and marshes.

However, the wildflower that grows most profusely in the open fields is not in the lily family. It is the Common Anemone or Poppy Anemone, and it can be found flowering from December through May in every hill and valley in Israel.

The Anemone appears in a variety of colours, ranging from scarlet, purple, and blue through to white. This beautiful flower belongs to the buttercup family, and the similarity of an open green field exhibiting wild buttercups and daisies is the placing of the Common Anemone.

It is this flower I personally feel that Jesus saw around Him when He mentioned the Lilies of the Field in what is known to us as 'The Sermon on the Mount'. The simplicity of their glorious adornment is easy to see and far outweighs the glory of Solomon.

The glory of Solomon is seen throughout the records of his life in all that he possessed, and all that he said, and all that he was. Another great person who seemingly had all the magnificent splendours of life, this being the Queen of Sheba, probably summed up this glory. Yet when she saw for herself the glory of Solomon, she was utterly overtaken with awe.

The magnificence of King Solomon had been reported to her, and clearly, she found it hard to believe, so much so that she made a journey of about 1,000 miles from Arabia to see for herself.

Jesus remarked upon the occasion, saying that she came from the 'uttermost parts of the earth to hear the wisdom of Solomon' (Matthew 12:42).

We read in I Kings 10:1–17 of her visit to Solomon to see his glory. What did she see? She saw his great wisdom, the magnificent house he had built, the splendid food on his table, his many obedient and loving servants, and his exquisite wardrobe. In her own words, upon seeing all the glories of Solomon, the Queen of Sheba said, 'behold, the half was not told me: your wisdom and prosperity exceeds the fame, which I heard.'

In all of this, Jesus, who declared Himself greater than Solomon, says in Matthew 12:42 that the glory of Solomon does not surpass the glory of the lilies of the field. What a statement to make! Why is this so?

The reason is simply that, although Solomon had been greatly blessed by God, all that he had was a product of man and his work, whereas the lilies of the field are the creative product of God, and nothing is more wonderful. Jesus is saying that even the small, seemingly insignificant things of life are more beautiful than any of the works of man.

So then let us again view the lilies of the field with new eyes and see the Glory of God. 'And why take ye thought for raiment? Consider the lilies of the field, how they grow; they toil not, neither do they spin: And yet I say unto you, that even Solomon in all his glory was not arrayed like one of these' (Matthew 6:28–29).

The Eagle

But they that wait upon the Lord shall renew their strength; they shall mount up with wings like eagles; they shall run, and not be weary; and they shall walk, and not faint. —Isaiah 40:31

As the lion is the king of the beasts, so is the eagle the king of the birds, and we shall see why this is so.

The Hebrew word for eagle is *Nesher*, meaning 'consecrated one', whereas the Greek is *Aetos*, meaning 'radiant one'. The Latin name for the eagle might tell us more; it is *Aquila Chrysaetos* – Golden Eagle'. Gold because of the golden colour sheen on its head.

There are many varieties of the eagle, but all have much the same characteristics. It can soar to much greater heights than other birds, which is why it is also known as the 'bird of heaven'.

All birds have a keen eye, but the eagle's eye is by far the sharpest and can look the sun full in the face. This is probably why it was made into the emblem of Saint John, symbolising an eye and insight into divine truth.

The eagle is a powerfully built bird with a strong beak, mighty talons, and a wingspan of over two metres. With these wings, the eagle can fly at speeds of 120–150 miles per hour and, amazingly, can dive on its prey at even greater speeds.

We find that the eagle is mentioned thirty-two times in the Bible, and some of these texts are worthy of note. In Exodus 19:4, we read of how the wings of the eagle symbolise the power of God in showing His support for the people of Israel.

Moses, in Deuteronomy 32:11–12, describes the action of the eagle over the nest of its young like unto the action of the Lord over His people, the eagle hovering over the nest, stirring up the young in it, and taking them upon its wings to fly away into safety.

The writer of Proverbs 30:18–19 says that, in his observation, there are four things that are very wonderful, and the first is the 'way of an eagle in the air'.

However, I think the best thoughts on the eagle are seen in Isaiah 40:31: 'But they that wait upon the Lord shall renew their strength; they shall mount up with wings as eagles; they shall run, and not be weary; and they shall walk, and not faint.'

No matter how strong or tough the path of life is, the promise is that the Lord will renew with strength like the eagle. At the height of an eagle in the sky, the believer similarly gets a viewpoint above everyone else.

At lower levels in the sky, the eagle is harassed by smaller birds, such as the crows and hawks, but because the eagle can soar so high, it can leave them all behind. Such is the victory for the Christian who can also rise above all others to leave the world behind, so to speak.

It is interesting to note that the remnant church of Israel, during the tribulation period, is given two wings of a great eagle that she might fly into the wilderness and escape. (See Revelation 12:14.)

The Christian should take careful note of the text in Isaiah and realise that being a believer does not automatically establish rights, such as rising high above all others. The key factor in the verse is the beginning, for it is only those who 'wait upon the Lord' who shall be likened to the eagle.

The reverse must be seen to be true in that those who do not take action will not have a renewal of strength.

Many countries throughout the world use the eagle as a national emblem, including Albania, Assyria, Egypt, Germany, Iraq, Poland, the United States, and many others. In fact, 119 national flags have eagles on them.

Do not forget that the eagle was the standard of the Roman Empire. Many would suppose this to be the reference Jesus makes in Matthew 24:28. He speaks about His coming again in the days of tribulation, when there will be great trouble in Israel, who is likened to the carcass, and the eagles are the troublesome nations gathered around. Nevertheless, the eagle is a creation of wonder that should not be passed over lightly when reading the scriptures.

The Bee

Behold, there was a swarm of bees and honey in the carcass of the lion. —Judges 14:8

Many small creatures are mentioned in the Bible, including insects. There is the ant, bee, flea, fly, gnat, grasshopper, hornet, locust, and moth, and we could include the spider on this list.

All of them have much to tell us, but there is something extra special about the bee. God created this creature to supply special food, which we of course know as honey.

As far as bees are concerned, we know them to be extremely industrious insects, and anyone with such a nature is affectionately called a 'busy bee'.

The first biblical mention of bees is in Deuteronomy 1:44, where the children of Israel, scattered by the Amorites, are likened to be as chased by bees, which I think is quite a vivid picture.

There is, of course, the popular story of Samson killing the lion and, upon returning to the carcass, finding a swarm of bees nesting in it with honey that they have made (Judges 14:5–9). It is interesting to note that forensic science today can establish time of death according to the body decomposition of the various species of insects found around the body at the time of discovery.

It is known that bees will not nest in a fresh carcass, but only when the bones are stripped and well dried. Scavengers of all types would feed on the dead lion first, followed by various insects. The bee does not feed off the lion but uses it as its home.

This means that Samson's lion carcass was very dry bones, which tells us that he spent some two to three months in Timnath with the woman before going home. This is more than we glean from the passage, which simply says, 'after a time he returned'.

No fewer than sixteen Old Testament texts refer to the new land of Israel, which was promised to the people of God, as a land 'flowing with milk and honey'.

The Psalmist speaks of the words of the Lord, which to him are even sweeter than honey in his mouth (Psalm 119:103). This is akin to the offer made by David in his Psalm 34:8: 'O taste and see that the Lord is good.'

The Proverb writer similarly remarks upon the fact that pleasant words are as a honeycomb, sweet to the soul and health to the bones (Proverbs 16:24). So it is that he gives the command to eat honey because it is good (Proverbs 24:13), but only so much, because the warning is there that too much of a good thing is bad for you and will make you sick (Proverbs 25:16).

The diet of John the Baptist consisted of locusts and wild honey (Matthew 3:4), and Jesus was given broiled fish and honeycomb to eat when He appeared to His disciples after His resurrection and asked for food to prove that He was flesh and bones (Luke 24:42).

What, then, is so special about the bee and its honey? It is not the purpose of this chapter to expound every attribute of the bee, for they are exceedingly manifold, but simply to reflect upon the bee's creative wonder. The structure of the honeycomb is in itself an architectural feat.

The honeybee that is seen flitting around the garden from flower to flower collects the nectar, returning it to the colony for processing into what we know as honey. Colony habitation brings about a way of life, and for the bee its way of life is very intricate.

The workload is shared by different types of bees; simply put, there are queens, workers, and drones. All the 'tradesmen' can be found in a colony, such as carpenters, miners, leaf cutters, guards, nurses, and undertakers.

No other creature is so organised in its life than the bee, and it is therefore truly a creation of wonder. 'Hast thou found honey? (Proverbs 25:16)

The Mustard Seed

The kingdom of heaven is like a grain of mustard seed, which a man took, and sowed in his field; Which indeed, is the least of all seeds; but when it is grown, it is the greatest among herbs, and becometh a tree, so that the birds of the air come and lodge in the branches of it. —Matthew 13:31–32

It has been the puzzlement of many that this mustard plant can grow into a tree large enough for birds to make their homes in. The real likelihood is that we are looking at two different species of plant.

Jesus speaks in His parable of a seed sown in the ground by man, but when it is grown, it is the greatest among the herbs. In illustrating it this way, it is a cultured herb from a very small seed, and in relation to its seed size does grow exceedingly large. However, it does not grow to the proportions of a tree in whose branches birds can lodge.

It is, however, also true that the mustard plant that we know in the north is not found in Israel. But there is a tree, known as *khardal,* that has a seed which is used as a substitute for mustard. *Khardal* is in fact the Arabic name for mustard.

It grows to the size of a large shrub or moderate-sized tree of about three metres and can be found in abundance around the river Jordan and Galilee, the very place where Jesus spoke of its worth in a parable.

The tree is actually called *Salvadora persica.* It has berries that are smaller than a grain of black pepper and a highly aromatic smell. It is because the seed is so small, yet not in fact literally the smallest of any seed, that it seems miraculous that it should be capable of growing into a tree, but this indeed is what it does, and Jesus, knowing this, uses it to illustrate the extent of faith.

The understanding of the parable is not for study here; we are particularly concerned with the mustard seed itself. Suffice to say that the information concerning the lodging of the birds in its branches is seen elsewhere in scripture. Ezekiel 17:23 and 31:6 tell of trees being great nations of glory but infiltrated by foreigners.

Daniel was asked to interpret Nebuchadnezzar's dream of a great tree that reached into heaven, with many dwelling in its shadows and boughs, yet the tree was cut down. This was interpreted as a mighty kingdom that would fall (Daniel chapter 4).

We can see a parallel with the parable of Jesus in that it foreshadows the Kingdom of Heaven growing as the church into such a world power that it becomes the nesting place of foreign creatures, that is, of different birds.

10

Read in the context of the whole passage, for this we must do, the surrounding parables that Jesus told speak of the bad being mixed with the good: tares and wheat, leaven and meal, and the dragnet of all kinds together.

All this is not to be confused with the subject matter of faith being as a grain of mustard seed. What indeed can be seen from illustrative uses of the mustard seed is that the very large can be born from the very little, and the mustard seed is used as a creation of wonder for this purpose.

Matthew 13:31 records the parable, and Matthew 17:20 records the faith.

The Rainbow

And the bow shall be in the cloud; and I will look upon it, that I may remember the everlasting covenant between God and every living creature of all flesh that is upon the earth. —Genesis 9:16

Everyone enjoys the sight of a rainbow in the sky after a rain shower. Technically and scientifically, we know that it is the rays of the sun being refracted through the rain droplets at different angles, and the thicker the rain cloud, the brighter the colours of the rainbow will be.

In school, we produced the same effect by passing light through a prism to dissipate the rays. We have discovered that, simply put, the rainbow contains seven colours: red, orange, yellow, green, blue, indigo, and violet. In this we begin to see the wonder of God's creation.

The rainbow is first encountered in scripture in Genesis 9:12–17, where we read about the end of Noah's flood. God said that He would set His bow in the sky as a covenant to man that He will never again flood the earth.

Before the flood, rain was not even a concept to man; there was only dew upon the ground to be seen every morning (Genesis 2:5–6). It could therefore be said that the rainbow in the sky did not and could not have existed before this time, yet the word *set* in the sky means 'to appoint' and suggests that the rainbow was always there and was probably seen as a result of the 'mist' that watered the earth. However, it matters not for our thoughts on the subject.

God said that the bow would be for a covenant, which is much more than just a promise. It is an agreement, and it is a two-way thing. The sign of the covenant is the rainbow through which God made His pledge, and it acts as a reminder of that pledge from God to man. When God speaks the word, it is done, and His word is profound.

God is merciful, and the rainbow is a symbol of His mercy so that, when the eyes see the rainbow, it reminds man's mind of God's heart towards him, that God spoke a pledge to him.

There is, however, a lot more to the rainbow that is worthy of note, comment, and thought. We have said that there are seven colours in this bow, and seven is the number of 'God in perfection'. It seems fitting, therefore, that the covenant pledge should be perfect.

Some have noticed that the Hebrew word for 'bow' is *qesheth,* which means a war-bow; Nevertheless, this war bow has become a symbol of peace, for there is no string to this bow, and no arrows can fly from it. There is to be no fighting anymore!

The rainbow appears elsewhere in scripture, but we should particularly note its appearance in Revelation 4:3. 'The one that sits upon the throne surrounded by the emerald-coloured rainbow is the Lord God in all His glory and completeness – Father, Son and Holy Spirit'. Here, the writer John records that the bow has an emerald green colour to it, and we should ask why this is so.

When we look back at the details concerning Israel's high priest in Exodus 28:15–21, we find an instruction to make a breastplate and inset it with twelve precious stones. Each stone represents a tribe of Israel. The fourth stone is the emerald, and, looking deeper, we find this represents the tribe of Judah. It is from the line of Judah that Jesus was born.

The emerald in the rainbow around the throne reveals that Christ is in the midst. As previously mentioned, the rainbow has seven colours and the middle colour is green, showing Christ in the midst.

In looking at the foundations of the wall of the Holy City in Revelation 21:19, it is written that the fourth stone is the emerald. Four is the number of the earth, and Christ is the one who rules over the earth. Green is the colour of freshness, new life, and, as shown in the rainbow around the throne, a new covenant.

So, the next time you see a rainbow, let it not remind you only of God's covenant with Noah but also that in the midst of its beauty is the Lord Jesus Christ, which is why the rainbow is a creation of wonder.

The Stars

He telleth the number of the stars; he calleth them all by their names. —Psalm 147:4

On the fourth day of creation, the sun, moon, and stars were created and set in the heavens to give light upon the earth. Since the beginning of time, man has been fascinated with the stars.

The scientist will tell us that the stars are formed by gravitational condensation of dust and various gases. This may be so, but they were nevertheless initially a creation of God. As far as the layman is concerned, a star is just a great ball of fire, of which the nearest to earth is the sun, and according to scientific measurement, most of them are many light years away from the earth.

The Bible refers to stars throughout its pages and speaks about different kinds of stars. There are the fixed stars that we know forming the constellations in the heavens, and from these constellations man has been reading the signs of the times.

The Babylonian people made much of 'reading the stars', yet they were shown to be foolish in following such 'magical' ways and fell under the judgement of God (Isaiah 47:13–14).

Job mentions some of the stars' names: Arcturus, Orion, and the Pleiades, which is a group of seven stars. There are millions of stars in the heavens, much beyond our comprehension, yet all are numbered and named by God according to the Psalmist (Psalm 147:4). They have been made for God's pleasure that they should praise Him.

There are stars that move, known as shooting stars or meteorites, as given in Revelation 6:13, and there are people in the Bible who are called stars – 'wise ones who shine with brightness' – in Daniel 12:3.

Then there are those stars which are God's angels, who are the guardians of the church (Revelation 1:20), stars that are referred to as good angels (Judges 5:20), and stars that are bad angels, particularly those led by Satan into rebellion against God (Revelation 12:4). The evilest star is known as Satan himself, called Lucifer and known as the 'son of the morning' or 'day star' in Isaiah 14:12.

In the New Testament, we see the special star that God sent to guide the Babylonian wise men from the east to Bethlehem (Matthew 2:1–10), for God used the minds of men for His own purpose, knowing that these magicians 'read' the signs of the constellations, for they were astrologers and stargazers.

These wise men knew about the reference to the 'star that shall come out of Jacob', given in the book of Numbers 24:17, and God caused a special star to appear in the constellation of Pisces the fish over the land of Judaea, the land which even today is symbolised by fishes. Thus God gave these wise men signs to follow in the stars that they might see and worship the true king of the world.

There is one star we haven't yet mentioned. It is referred to as the 'morning star' by Peter, and the verse is worth quoting in full here: 'We have the word of the prophets made more certain, and you will do well to pay attention to it, as to a light shining in a dark place, until the day dawns and the morning star rises in your hearts' (II Peter 1:19 [NIV]). But what is this star that will arise in our hearts?

According to Revelation 2:26–28, the morning star is a gift for the believer, and the gift of this morning star in Revelation 22:16 being none other than Christ's own declaration of Himself to be 'the root and offspring of David, the bright and morning star'. The star spoken about was to be 'out of Jacob from the tribe of Judah in Israel'.

It can truly be said then that of all the stars in the universe, which are creations of wonder, the greatest above them all is the creator Himself, Jesus Christ. *And* if you want to follow the stars, then read the stars of the Bible, for it is there that you will find the truth for your life.

The Teardrop

Jesus wept. —John 11:35

Tears are the outward signs of inner feelings, and we would therefore do well to take note when we see them. They are, of course, shed for many different reasons. But first, what are tears?

Tears are clear, salty fluids that flow from the socket of the eye. They are secreted from a gland in each eye. Tears are principally used to lubricate the eyes and eyelids. Each tear gland, called a lacrimal gland, is almond in shape and about half its size. From this gland there are ducts that transport the fluid to the surface of the eye.

In normal working practice, this secretion is small and spreads evenly over the surface of the eye, which then drains away into a sac by the side of the nose, where it eventually evaporates.

When this fluid becomes excessive, it spills out of the nose and over the lower eyelids, running down the cheeks as tears. The causes of this excess are many, which, apart from irritation, such as a foreign body entering the eyes, range from a feeling of happiness to one of sadness.

The Bible has very many examples of tears being shed, and in Psalm 120:5–6, we see tears as seeds to be sown. As with any harvest, we reap what we sow, for if we sow plenty, we will reap plenty. Distress in a person's life does not last forever; it is merely a means to an end.

Sorrow is sowing the seed and rejoicing in the reaping that follows. The one who rejoices over a lost soul is usually the one who has wept much and shed tears for that soul. A new birth does not come without pain.

God said in Psalm 120 that rejoicing is doubtless a result of the sowing. We therefore should have no doubts because the Lord has said the rejoicing will happen. When the earthly pots were filled with water, Jesus turned them into wine, and when the earthly eyes are also filled with water, then does Jesus turn them into wine of joy.

Isaiah shed tears of anxiety for his people; he saw the problems as a day of trouble (Isaiah 22:4–5). Jeremiah was known as the weeping prophet, not because he was of a miserable or weak disposition but because of his anxiety for the state of God's people (Jeremiah 9:1, 18–19; 13:17; and 14:17).

Jesus shed tears over a city that was lost and far away from the truth, yet He longed that it should return to God and receive peace instead of trouble (Luke 19:41–42). Paul similarly had anxious thoughts and wept for the safety of his loved ones (Acts 20:31).

The torment of Job showed in the tears that he shed in such volume that his visage was not a pretty sight (Job 16:16). David's grief and tears made him weary upon his bed, but he knew that the Lord was close by (Psalm 6).

How the tears of rejection came into the eyes of Esau when he witnessed the blessing of his father Isaac upon his brother Jacob. He begs of his father, 'Hast thou but one blessing, my father? Bless me, even me also, O my father'. (Genesis 27:38).

The repentance of King Hezekiah through tears brought reconciliation with God and extended his lifespan by fifteen years (II Kings 20:3). When Jesus's foretelling that Peter would deny Him finally came to pass, Peter wept bitterly (Luke 22:62).

Not all weeping found in the Bible is for sadness. For example, there is the occasion when the foundations of the temple had been laid in the rebuilding programme, and the people rejoiced greatly and wept for joy (Ezra 3:10–13).

The love that the sinful woman had for Jesus was such that, as she wept, her tears washed His feet, and she dried them with her hair. Jesus saw her heart and showed appreciation for her compassion (Luke 7:37–50).

The shortest verse in the Bible is simply 'Jesus wept'; tears of utter compassion moved in His heart and spirit so deeply that he displayed His emotions (John 11:35).

The accounts of weeping in the Bible are manifold but let us concern ourselves with the weeping in heaven and hell. Jesus said that in hell, there would be not just weeping but wailing and gnashing of teeth.

This is crying most bitterly in great anguish. Why will this be? It will be because those who are there in 'outer darkness' and in the 'lake of fire' will be lost from God. The opportunity to dwell with God eternally will have been lost, and so a great weeping by many will abound (Matthew 13:49–50).

Contrast this with the weeping in heaven; when we read the Bible, we find that there will be none. John, in his writing of the Revelation of Jesus Christ, tells us what he saw at the very end of days. He saw a new heaven and a new earth. He saw a new city of God, and in this city dwelt the people of God.

Then, the wonderful verse of Revelation 21:4 says, 'And God shall wipe away all tears from their eyes; and there shall be no more death, neither sorrow, nor crying, neither shall there be any more pain: for the former things are passed away.'

Surely then we can say that just a mere teardrop is a creation of wonder, for it expresses so much in life, until the day arrives that such expression of the sad and painful tear will no longer be seen.

The Sea

Thou rulest the raging of the sea; when the waves thereof arise, thou stillest them. —Psalm 89:9

In the beginning of earth's creation, there was no sea. We read in the first chapter of Genesis that God's separation of the waters above the heavens from those below the heavens brought these waters below the heavens together in one place, and He called the dry land *earth* and the waters He called *seas*. This is the creation of the seas that occurred on the third day.

On the sixth day, God created man and gave him dominion over everything on the earth, including the sea, but notice that He did not give dominion over the heavens (Genesis 1:38).

Man has explored virtually every corner of the earth and has now set out to explore the heavens and the universe, where he has no dominion, although he has yet to plumb the depths of the seas.

God made the sea, and thereupon He, and not Britannia, rules over the raging waves (Psalm 89:9). He has the power of the winds over the sea, as we see in the time of Jonah when he tried to run away from God. Jesus also holds this power, as we see when He rebuked the wind and the waves when the storm arose (Matthew 8:26). As observed by Solomon in Ecclesiastes 1:7, He causes the rivers to run into the seas.

Great events have taken place in the seas. We may think particularly of the time when the Red Sea was parted so the Hebrew people could pass over to the other side, whilst their pursuers drowned when the waves rolled back over them (Exodus 14:21–30).

What greater demonstration of power over the sea could be given than when Jesus, the Son of God, walked not *through* it, but *on* it in Matthew 14:25–27?

There are, however, other aspects of the sea to consider that cause wonder. We find that it is in the depth of the sea that the Lord puts our sins, according to Micah 7:19, and that is something important to remember, as we shall see later.

In the Revelation of Jesus Christ, as given to John on the Isle of Patmos, we learn much about the sea in the end days. There will come a time in these end days when God sends destruction upon the world as we know it today, but before this happens, the believers of God will be set aside and protected from the mighty calamities that will be poured out.

We see an instruction given to an angel sent from God not to hurt the earth or the sea until His people have been protected (Revelation 7:2–3). Then we read further on that the angel pours out troubles upon the sea, and all that are in it at the time will die (Revelation 16:3).

Now let us move further on in these last days, when we read about the final judgement of mankind and note especially those who died in the sea, for the sea will give up its dead that they will stand before the throne of judgement (Revelation 20:12–13).

The next observation of John is particularly worthy of note in that he sees a new heaven and a new earth, for the present ones have passed away – and there is no more sea (Revelation 21:1) – no more sea and no more of the sins that it contained.

Our question is, why should this be? For some answers, we need to go back to Genesis 3:17, where we read that because Adam sinned by disobedience, the earth was cursed. This curse became so great in time that God caused the earth to be covered by the sea in the days of Noah.

The Man

And God said, let us make man in our image, after our likeness; and let them have dominion over the fish of the sea, and over the fowl of the air, and over the cattle, and over all the earth, and over every creeping thing that creepeth upon the earth. —Genesis 1:26

The creation of man is without a doubt the most wonderful of God's mighty hand. We find in the Genesis story of creation that having spent five days in forming the world and all that is in it, the culmination on the sixth day would be the best.

We find it not uncommon in our own lives to leave the best until the end, but why did God choose this format? Clearly, we must say that we do not know the mind of God in such things, but we do know that man is the image and glory of God (I Corinthians 11:7).

God said, after all the good things that He had made, 'let us make man in our image, after our likeness' (Genesis 1:26). If we read the scriptures carefully, we will find that nothing else is made in the image and likeness of God, so what is his image like?

First, we must say that the image is not physical likeness, for God is not flesh but spirit (John 4:24). The image and likeness are therefore of a spiritual nature, possessing all the attributes and characteristics of God.

The Bible is absolutely and distinctively clear that God is a triune God; my purpose is not to prove that here, but Father, Son, and Holy Spirit are the three persons that are God.

If God is a trinity, then it follows that man is also a trinity because he is made in His image and likeness. The Bible again confirms this, saying that we are made of body, soul, and spirit. Paul, in his letter to the Thessalonians (5:23), says, 'I pray God your whole spirit and soul and body be preserved blameless.'

The writer to the Hebrews in chapter 4 v 12 tells us that the word of God divides the soul and spirit, and the joints and marrow (which is the body).

If we now return to Genesis 2:7, we can clearly understand the creation of man as a trinity. The verse tells us that man was formed from the dust of the ground (the body), that what was breathed into him was life (the spirit), and he became a living soul. We have already established that the spirit and soul are separate entities and are not, and cannot be, one and the same.

The picture that many have of God creating a body and animating it by breathing air into its lungs is absurd. Man could do that, but the end result would not bring life into the body. Remember, God is a spirit, and spirits do not have bodies nor need lungs in which to exert air. What God the spirit breathed was the spirit of life.

Notice the material that God used to make man's body: it was no more that the dust of the ground. The dust was worthless. It was not even gold dust, neither was it a good vegetable loam, but just dust of no value and of the kind that is sucked up into a vacuum cleaner. Man has said in his wisdom that 'you cannot make a silk purse out of a sow's ear', but God can and does!

James 2:26 says that the body without the spirit is dead. Solomon tells us in Ecclesiastes 12:7 that, at death, 'the dust shall return to the earth as it was; and the spirit shall return unto God who gave it.'

The soul is the most interesting part of man because his eternal life depends on it. Ezekiel 18:20 tells us that 'The soul that sinneth, it shall die'. Sin is merely a transgression of God's laws, and if the soul turns away from God the life-giver, then it will die. In other words, come and listen to God the life-giver, and you (your soul) will live. The Psalmist says in Psalm 119:175, 'let my soul live, and it shall praise thee.'

It is our souls that need to be saved. Our natural bodies will die and return to dust; the spirit of life within us will return to God who gave it, for that part breathed from God cannot die; and our souls will go to either heaven or hell according to the decisions we make. God does not decide which of these places our soul shall belong to; we do.

It is not God's wish that any soul should perish in hell, for He would have us all be saved. The problem is merely one of cleanness. God is all clean, and the soul within a man who sins becomes unclean. The clean cannot mix with the unclean, lightness cannot mix with darkness.

The solution is that the unclean must be made clean. No amount of self-washing will do this, for the unclean does not have the power to make itself clean. Cleaning needs an external agent, and this external agent is none other than His Son Jesus Christ, for He as a man committed no sin and was always perfectly clean.

The reality of what God did was to make man clean again by paying the penalty for all of man's wrongdoing, or sins, by putting them upon the soul of the innocent and perfect man Jesus Christ. This is the reason the Son of God died on the cross, to save our souls from paying the penalty for our sins, and thus man is made clean again.

The answer to the saving of our souls has graciously been given to us by God the creator to decide our own destiny. If we accept that Jesus died on the cross for our sins, rose again from the grave because death could not hold the sinless one, believe this in our hearts, and confess with our mouths, we (our souls) will be saved (Romans 10:9).

Conversely, if we reject God's plan for saving our souls, then we are damned. There is only one way back to God, and that is through Jesus Christ His son (John 14:6).

The complexity of man (and we have not even touched upon his physical form) and all that God has put into him is the ultimate creation of wonder.

The Cross

And he, bearing his cross, went forth into a place called 'The place of a skull', which is called in the Hebrew, Golgotha, Where they crucified him, and two others with him, on either side one, and Jesus in the midst. —John 19:17–18.

We have read about just a few of God's creations, and all are truly wonderful, but in closing, let us look at a creation of man.

When man disobeyed God in the Garden of Eden, he started down a road that led to destruction, a downward path so far away from his Creator. After just 1,500 years, at the time of Noah, man had become so depraved that God had seen enough and decided to destroy all He had made (Genesis 6:5–7).

The imagination and thoughts of man's heart were continually evil, and Jeremiah says that the heart is deceitful above all things and desperately wicked (Jeremiah 17:9). Fortunately, there was one good man called Noah, and but for him, all would have indeed been destroyed. Genesis 6:8 says, 'But Noah found grace in the eyes of the Lord.'

Throughout the ages, as we can easily read in our history books, man has shown himself to be, at one end, a master and genius, yet at the other extremity, his cruelty is unsurpassed by anything else in creation. The suffering, pain, and torture man has inflicted upon his fellow men is almost beyond belief, but we know it to be true.

The types of torture and death that man has imposed have been manifold, but none, I believe, is eviler than crucifixion. Most instruments of death, such as beheading with an axe, sword, or guillotine, are quick. The gun, the electric chair, the gas chamber, and lethal injection are also swift. Stoning takes a little longer, as does the ducking chair.

Being hung is reasonably quick but, when coupled with being drawn and quartered, is horrendous. However, no form of execution surpasses crucifixion for the torment it causes, which can last for three days before the victim finally dies. And of all the above, how many are instruments of torture and death that are carried by the victim? Those that would be crucified would very often carry their own cross upon which they would be nailed.

The first record of crucifixion came from the Persian Empire in about 519 BC. Alexander the Great brought it into the Greek Empire and thus into the Roman Empire through the Carthaginians.

There were many different kinds of crosses, but they primarily fell into one of two types. The first consisted of an upright post, called a *stipes,* with a cross piece, called a *patibulum,* across the top, forming the capital letter T and known as the Tau cross after the Greek letter tau. Most archaeological evidence points towards the Tau cross as the cross of Jesus.

The traditional cross that we think of, known as the Latin cross, consists of the cross piece being positioned farther down the post, forming a lower-case t shape.

It is thought that the Latin cross would be too heavy even for a strong, healthy man to carry, adding further weight to the argument that Jesus was crucified on a Tau cross. With a Tau cross, the victim carries only the *patibulum*, which was quite heavy enough, weighing about 60kg. The *stipes* would already be in the ground at the place of execution.

The fixing of the victim to the cross by nailing hands and feet was not the original form. The early form was to nail the feet but only to tie the hands to the cross piece, but this simply took too long, and the agony for the victim was not considered to be enough.

There was a time also that a saddle, called a *sedile,* was fixed to the cross for the victim to rest upon when he began to tire. This was a pointed piece of wood that gave little comfort, but it was abandoned because it hindered the real aspect of the torture.

Victims were fixed to the cross by nails hammered through the wrist bones; nails driven through the palms would only tear away through the fingers and would not support the body weight. The feet were placed together, one over the other, and a nail was driven through the arches of each foot into the timber behind.

Crucifixion victims' arms were not pulled straight, but hung loose, and the legs were not fully straight but bent at the knees. This position allowed the victim to rise and fall between his fixings. The sagging of the hanging body caused great pain on the wrists, and if the victim raised himself up to relieve the pain, he pressed up from the nails in his feet, causing equally great pain in his feet.

The physical and mental pain of being crucified was excruciating, knowing that only death could end it. But the victim had no means of hastening death to relieve the agony. Eventually, there would come a point when there was no more strength left in the body to lift itself, and the body just hung by the arms.

The common method applied to end a crucifixion was to break the legs so that the victim would be unable to lift himself up. He would suffocate quickly because air could be drawn into the lungs but not exhaled, and the build-up of carbon dioxide in the lungs caused the victim to die.

Crucifixion was undertaken carefully so that it usually lasted for many hours, but in the case of Jesus Christ, He was already severely weakened by the scourging and beatings previously received. As I mentioned, the common way to end a crucifixion was to break the legs, but in the case of Jesus, this was not done because they found He was already dead. To make sure, a spear was driven up through His chest into His heart, thus causing the flow of water from around the heart and the blood from the heart itself to pour out.

Is not therefore the cross a creation of wonder against man?

When we see the wonderful and beautiful creations of God and then see just how far man has removed himself from his Creator, it is difficult to understand why God does not bring it all to an end now.

However, the love and grace of God is all-sufficient, allowing man the opportunity to turn from his ways and come back to his Creator, until one day, of course, when there will come a reckoning, and man will be seen to have judged himself.

About the Author

Alex Frame became a Christian at the age of 17 in 1962 and has been a Bible student since then. He taught for many years as a Bible teacher and pastor. This is just one of the many teaching books that he has written, and he believes that the Bible holds many truths that are there to be discovered and passed on.

His books include the following titles:

Shadows of Jesus Christ in the Old Testament

Hard Passages of the Bible

Reasons (Guide to Modern Issues and Bible Wisdom) - 3 Volumes

95 Miles on a Donkey (Journey of Mary and Joseph)

Death at Calvary (Who was Responsible)

He is a chartered surveyor by profession.

The most precious thing that he has is the life that God gave to him.